MW01016484

foreword

A blender is a handy little appliance. Toss in a few choice ingredients, push the button and voilà! You have a tasty, refreshing drink.

The simple recipes in this handy collection feature ingredients you might not have thought of adding to a drink. Peanut butter and amaranth in a smoothie? You bet. Homemade Irish Cream? Beats store-bought any day.

You'll find a drink for every occasion and every palate. Kids and adults alike will love the selection of nutritious fruit and vegetable smoothies for a quick, healthy snack or breakfast on the go. Want something special after a rough day at work? Whip up a creamy Coffee Alexander Shake or an evening cocktail. And there is something for every season, from cool refreshments for your summer barbecue to warm liquid hugs that chase away the bitter winter chill.

Jean Paré

citrus shake

Silky papaya with the tang of grapefruit and orange.

Ruby red grapefruit juice	1 cup	250 mL
Chopped papaya	1 cup	250 mL
Vanilla frozen yogurt	1 cup	250 mL
Frozen concentrated orange juice	2 tbsp.	30 mL

Process all 4 ingredients in blender until smooth. Pour into 2 medium glasses. Makes about 2 1/2 cups (625 mL). Serves 2.

1 serving: 239 Calories; 4.5 g Total Fat (1.3 g Mono, 0.2 g Poly, 2.7 g Sat); 2 mg Cholesterol; 47 g Carbohydrate; 2 g Fibre; 5 g Protein; 72 mg Sodium

coconut fruit smoothie

A great breakfast drink to jump-start the morning. Treat yourself to a taste of the tropics.

Ripe large mango	1	1
(about 12 oz., 340 g), chopped		
Fresh (or whole frozen) strawberries	10	10
Medium banana, cut up	1	1
(see Tip, page 64)		
Orange juice	1 cup	250 mL
Light coconut milk	1 cup	250 mL

Put all 5 ingredients into blender. Process until smooth. Makes about 4 cups (1 L).

1 cup (250 mL): 140 Calories; 4.5 g Total Fat (0 g Mono, 0 g Poly, 3 g Sat); 0 mg Cholesterol; 25 g Carbohydrate; 2 g Fibre; 1 g Protein; 15 mg Sodium

malted banana shake

Use ripe bananas to make this creamy, chocolatey drink even better!

Medium bananas (see Tip, page 64)	2	2
Malted milk drink powder (such as Ovaltine)	3 tbsp.	45 mL
Frozen vanilla yogurt	2/3 cup	150 mL
Chocolate milk	2 cups	500 mL

Cocoa, sifted if lumpy, sprinkle

Put first 4 ingredients into blender. Process until smooth.

Sprinkle cocoa over individual servings. Makes 4 cups (1 L).

1 cup (250 mL): 180 Calories; 2.5 g Total Fat (0 g Mono, 0 g Poly, 1.5 g Sat); 10 mg Cholesterol; 10 g Carbohydrate; 2 g Fibre; 7 g Protein; 125 mg Sodium

blueberry lemonade smoothie

Tangy lemon and sweet blueberries combine in a light smoothie that is perfect for chasing away the summer heat.

Frozen blueberries	1 cup	250 mL
Milk	2/3 cup	150 mL
Frozen concentrated lemonade	6 tbsp.	90 mL
Ice cubes	6	6

Put all 4 ingredients into blender. Process until smooth. Pour into 2 glasses. Makes 3 1/2 cups (875 mL). Serves 2.

1 serving: 178 Calories; 2.3 g Total Fat (0 g Mono, trace Poly, 1 g Sat); 7 mg Cholesterol; 39 g Carbohydrate; 2 g Fibre; 3 g Protein; 44 mg Sodium

apricot breakfast drink

Golden and creamy, with a frothy layer on top. A satisfying start to your day!

Can of apricot halves in light syrup (14 oz., 398 mL), with syrup	1	1
Ice cubes	16	16
Milk	1 cup	250 mL
Low-fat plain yogurt	1/2 cup	125 mL
Liquid honey	2 tbsp.	30 mL
Ground nutmeg	1/8 tsp.	0.5 mL

Process all 6 ingredients in blender until smooth. Pour into 3 large glasses. Makes about 5 cups (1.25 L). Serves 3.

1 serving: 173 Calories; 1.1 g Total Fat (0.3 g Mono, 0.1 g Poly, 0.6 g Sat); 4 mg Cholesterol; 38 g Carbohydrate; 1 g Fibre; 6 g Protein; 79 mg Sodium

mango almond smoothie

Super simple and full of protein. Frozen fruit adds a creamy element to this power-packed smoothie.

Frozen mango pieces	**3 cups**	**750 mL**
Vanilla soy milk, chilled	**2 cups**	**500 mL**
Can of sliced peaches	**1**	**1**
(14 oz., 398 mL), with juice		
Almond butter	**1/4 cup**	**60 mL**

Process all 4 ingredients in blender or food processor until smooth. Makes about 6 cups (1.5 L).

Serves 6.

1 cup (250 mL): 170 Calories; 7 g Total Fat (0 g Mono, 0.5 g Poly, 0.5 g Sat); 0 mg Cholesterol; 23 g Carbohydrate; 3 g Fibre; 5 g Protein; 45 mg Sodium

rainforest smoothie

The açaí berry is the fruit of the açaí palm, which grows in Central and South America. It looks rather like a grape and is renowned for its high levels of antioxidants. Açaí purée can be found in your local health food store, and it is also available online.

Açaí purée or juice (frozen or thawed)	7 oz.	200 g
Mango, chopped	1	1
Chopped papaya	1 cup	250 mL
Coconut water (see Tip, page 64) or papaya juice	1 cup	250 mL

Combine all 4 ingredients in blender. Purée until smooth. Divide among 2 glasses. Serves 2.

1 serving: 180 Calories; 2.5 g Total Fat (0 g Mono, 0 g Poly, 0 g Sat); 0 mg Cholesterol; 43 g Carbohydrate; 5 g Fibre; 2 g Protein; 135 mg Sodium

mixed berry smoothie

The goji berry comes from the Himalayas and is a highly nutritious berry with a long history of use in China. In North America, it is generally found in a dry form, much like a raisin.

Goji berries	1/2 cup	125 mL
Orange juice	1 cup	250 mL
Blackberries	1/2 cup	125 mL
Raspberries	1/2 cup	125 mL
Blueberries	1/2 cup	125 mL
Strawberries	1/2 cup	125 mL
Apple, chopped	1	1
Bee pollen	2 tsp.	10 mL

Place goji berries in small bowl. Add orange juice and set aside to hydrate for about 1 hour.

Transfer mixture to blender. Add berries and apple. Purée until smooth. Divide among 2 glasses. Sprinkle each glass with 1 tsp. (5 mL) bee pollen. Serves 2.

1 serving: 270 Calories; 2 g Total Fat (0 g Mono, 0.5 g Poly, 0 g Sat); 0 mg Cholesterol; 64 g Carbohydrate; 10 g Fibre; 7 g Protein; 55 mg Sodium

berry bran shake

Breakfast in a glass! The natural sweetness of fruit gets a boost from raisin bran to make a filling breakfast beverage.

Frozen whole strawberries, cut up	2 cups	500 mL
Milk	2 cups	500 mL
Raisin bran cereal	1/2 cup	125 mL
Chopped pitted dates (see Tip, page 64)	1/4 cup	60 mL

Process all 4 ingredients in blender or food processor for about 3 minutes until smooth. Makes about 4 cups (1 L).

1 cup (250 mL): 132 Calories; 1.8 g Total Fat (0.4 g Mono, 0.2 g Poly, 0.9 g Sat); 5 mg Cholesterol; 26 g Carbohydrate; 4 g Fibre; 5 g Protein; 109 mg Sodium

wake-up call

A little bit of tea, some protein and plenty of fruit make this drink a healthy and delicious breakfast to have on the go.

Vanilla soy milk	1 cup	250 mL
Green tea bags	2	2
(fruit flavoured or plain)		
Ripe medium banana, cut into	1	1
1/2 inch (12 mm) slices,		
partially frozen (see Tip, page 64)		
Frozen (or fresh) strawberries, cut into	1 cup	250 mL
1/2 inch (12 mm) slices,		
partially frozen		
Liquid honey	2 tbsp.	30 mL

Heat and stir soy milk in small saucepan on high for about 4 minutes until boiling. Add tea bags. Cover. Let steep for 5 minutes. Squeeze and discard tea bags. Pour into 2 cup (500 mL) liquid measure. Chill.

Put banana and strawberries into blender. Add honey and tea mixture. Process until smooth. Makes 2 cups (500 mL).

1 cup (250 mL): 219 Calories; 3.6 g Total Fat (0.6 g Mono, 1.7 g Poly, 0.6 g Sat); 0 mg Cholesterol; 45 g Carbohydrate; 3 g Fibre; 5 g Protein; 71 mg Sodium

green chill

Sweet and delicious. A great way to sneak a bit of spinach into your diet—the sweetness of the fruit masks the spinach, but you still reap the nutritional benefits!

Vanilla soy milk	1 1/2 cups	375 mL
Frozen pineapple chunks	1/2 cup	125 mL
Apple chunks, peel on	1/2 cup	125 mL
Chopped spinach	1/2 cup	125 mL
Agave syrup	1 tbsp.	15 mL
Apple juice	1/4 cup	60 mL

Combine first 5 ingredients in blender. Process until smooth, adding apple juice if the mixture is too thick. Serves 2.

1 serving: 170 Calories; 3 g Total Fat (1 g Mono, 1.5 g Poly, 0 g Sat); 0 mg Cholesterol; 30 g Carbohydrate; 3 g Fibre; 6 g Protein; 250 mg Sodium

gazpacho smoothie

If you enjoy vegetable cocktail drinks, you're going to love this savoury, refreshing smoothie loaded with all the flavours of the popular Spanish soup.

Chopped English cucumber (with peel)	2 cups	250 mL
Can of diced tomatoes (14 oz., 398 mL), with juice	1	1
Unsweetened applesauce	1/2 cup	125 mL
Chopped red pepper	1/4 cup	60 mL
Chopped fresh cilantro (or parsley)	1 tbsp.	15 mL
Pepper	1/4 tsp.	1 mL
Garlic powder	1/8 tsp.	0.5 mL
Onion powder	1/8 tsp.	0.5 mL
Hot pepper sauce (optional)		

Process all 9 ingredients in blender until smooth. Makes about 3 1/3 cups (825 mL). Serves 4.

1 serving: 40 Calories; 0 g Total Fat (0 g Mono, 0 g Poly, 0 g Sat); 0 mg Cholesterol; 10 g Carbohydrate; 1 g Fibre; 1 g Protein; 310 mg Sodium

strawberry carrot smoothie

Get your day off to a good start with this thick, creamy and not-too-sweet smoothie. You could cook extra carrots at dinnertime so you're all ready to go in the morning.

Chopped carrot	2 cups	500 mL
Frozen overripe medium banana, cut up (see Tip, page 64)	1	1
Whole frozen strawberries	1 cup	250 mL
Milk	3/4 cup	175 mL
Vanilla yogurt	3/4 cup	175 mL
Liquid honey	2 tsp.	10 mL

Pour water into small saucepan until about 1 inch (2.5 cm) deep. Add carrot. Cover. Bring to a boil. Reduce heat to medium. Boil gently for about 10 minutes until tender. Drain. Plunge into ice water in medium bowl. Let stand for about 10 minutes until cold. Drain. Transfer to blender or food processor.

Add remaining 5 ingredients. Process until smooth. Makes about 3 1/2 cups (875 mL). Serves 4.

1 serving: 130 Calories; 2.5 g Total Fat (0 g Mono, 0 g Poly, 1 g Sat); 5 mg Cholesterol; 26 g Carbohydrate; 3 g Fibre; 5 g Protein; 105 mg Sodium

lime cucumber lassi

An Indian beverage, lassi comes in sweet and savoury varieties. The refreshing coolness of yogurt, lime and cucumber makes this savoury version a must-try for a hot day.

Chopped peeled English cucumber, seeds removed	1 1/2 cups	375 mL
Plain yogurt	1 cup	250 mL
Sour cream	1 cup	250 mL
Crushed ice	1/2 cup	125 mL
Milk	1/2 cup	125 mL
Liquid honey	2 tsp.	10 mL
Lime juice	1 tsp.	5 mL
Grated lime zest	1/4 tsp.	1 mL
Ground cumin	1/4 tsp.	1 mL
Ground ginger	1/4 tsp.	1 mL
Salt, sprinkle		

English cucumber slices (with peel), for garnish

Process first 11 ingredients in blender or food processor until smooth. Pour into 4 glasses.

Garnish with cucumber slices. Makes about 4 1/2 cups (1.1 L).

1 cup (250 mL): 169 Calories; 10 g Total Fat (0.1 g Mono, trace Poly, 7 g Sat); 42 mg Cholesterol; 10 g Carbohydrate; trace Fibre; 6 g Protein; 71 mg Sodium

mocha coffee

Why pay coffee shop prices when you can make your own version at home? This handy mix can be stored in the cupboard for up to 6 months. Just pull it out and add it to a mug of hot water when you are in the mood for a gourmet coffee. Add whipped cream, a sprinkle of cinnamon and perhaps a few chocolate curls for a decadent treat.

Skim milk powder	2/3 cup	150 mL
Granulated sugar	2/3 cup	150 mL
Instant coffee granules	1/2 cup	125 mL
Powdered coffee whitener	1/4 cup	60 mL
Cocoa	1/4 cup	60 mL

Measure first 5 ingredients into blender. Pulse to make more powdery. Makes 1 1/2 cups (375 mL) mix, enough for 18 servings.

To make a serving of coffee, measure 4 tsp. (20 mL) into 1 cup (250 mL) boiling water in mug. Stir. Garnish with dollop of whipped cream and a sprinkle of cinnamon or chocolate curls, if desired.

1 serving: 50 Calories; 0.5 g Total Fat (0 g Mono, 0 g Poly, 0.5 g Sat); 0 mg Cholesterol; 11 g Carbohydrate; 0 g Fibre; 1 g Protein; 15 mg Sodium

maple iced coffee

Thick and creamy maple-flavoured dessert coffee. Serve with a spoon or straw.

Cold strong prepared coffee (see Tip, page 64)	**1 1/2 cups**	**375 mL**
Maple (or vanilla) ice cream, softened	**1 cup**	**250 mL**
Maple (or maple-flavoured) syrup	**2 tbsp.**	**30 mL**
Ice cubes	**6**	**6**

Process all 4 ingredients in blender until smooth. Makes about 2 cups (500 mL). Pour into 2 chilled medium glasses. Serves 2.

1 serving: 200 Calories; 7.7 g Total Fat (2.2 g Mono, 0.3 g Poly, 4.7 g Sat); 31 mg Cholesterol; 31 g Carbohydrate; 0 g Fibre; 3 g Protein; 65 mg Sodium

coffee alexander shake

A variation of a favourite cocktail. Add a dollop of whipped cream and sprinkle of chocolate curls for a quick finishing touch. For a more authentic Coffee Alexander, add 1/4 cup (60 mL) brandy.

Boiling water	1/4 cup	60 mL
Instant coffee granules	2 tsp.	10 mL
Milk	1 cup	250 mL
Chocolate syrup	2 tbsp.	30 mL
Vanilla ice cream	1 cup	250 mL

Stir boiling water and coffee granules in small cup. Cool.

Put milk, syrup, ice cream and prepared coffee into blender. Process until smooth. Pour into 2 fancy stemware glasses. Makes 2 cups (500 mL). Serves 2.

1 serving: 260 Calories; 9 g Total Fat (2 g Mono, 0 g Poly, 6 g Sat); 35 mg Cholesterol; 37 g Carbohydrate; 1 g Fibre; 8 g Protein; 150 mg Sodium

orange frostbite

Smooth and frothy—just right for summer! Use "glasses" made from whole oranges for a fun presentation, but be sure to freeze them for at least 2 hours before filling. For a child-friendly frostbite, leave out the liqueur.

ORANGE DREAM LIQUEUR

Water	1/2 cup	125 mL
Granulated sugar	1/4 cup	60 mL
Vodka	3/4 cup	175 mL
Can of sweetened condensed milk (11 oz., 300 mL)	1/2	1/2
Frozen concentrated orange juice	2 1/2 tbsp.	37 mL
Vanilla	1 tsp.	5 mL
Medium oranges, peeled, seeds and white pith removed	4	4
Vanilla ice cream	1 3/4 cups	425 mL

Orange Dream Liqueur: Measure water and sugar into small saucepan. Bring to a boil on medium. Heat and stir until sugar is dissolved. Remove from heat. Let stand until cooled completely.

Measure next 4 ingredients into blender. Add sugar mixture. Process for about 1 minute until smooth. Set aside.

Cut oranges into quarters. Place in blender.

Add ice cream and 1/2 cup (125 mL) liqueur. (Pour remaining liqueur into sterile glass jar with tight-fitting lid and store for up to 1 month in refrigerator.) Process until smooth. Makes about 4 cups (1 L). Pour into 4 chilled medium glasses. Serves 4.

1 serving: 266 Calories; 7.9 g Total Fat (2.3 g Mono, 0.3 g Poly, 4.8 g Sat); 31 mg Cholesterol; 41 g Carbohydrate; 2 g Fibre; 4 g Protein; 65 mg Sodium

berry citrus freeze

Strawberry and orange with a lime tang. Refreshing without being overly sweet. To dress up this drink, dampen the rims of the glasses with lime wedge and press them into coloured sugar until coated.

Frozen whole strawberries, chopped	2 cups	500 mL
Orange juice	1 1/2 cups	375 mL
Strawberry ice cream topping	1/4 cup	60 mL
Lime juice	3 tbsp.	45 mL
Tequila	6 tbsp.	90 mL
Orange-flavoured liqueur (such as Grand Marnier)	3 tbsp.	45 mL

Process first 4 ingredients in blender until smooth. Pour into 2 quart (2 L) shallow baking dish. Cover. Freeze for about 2 hours until almost firm.

Scrape strawberry mixture, using fork, into blender. Add tequila and liqueur. Process until smooth. Makes about 3 1/2 cups (875 mL). Pour into 4 chilled small glasses. Serves 4.

1 serving: 219 Calories; 0.4 g Total Fat (0.1 g Mono, 0.1 g Poly, 0 g Sat); 0 mg Cholesterol; 37 g Carbohydrate; 2 g Fibre; 1 g Protein; 9 mg Sodium

citrus sunburst

A refreshing, eye-catching drink, bursting with orange flavour.

CITRUS CREAM

Orange sherbet	2 cups	500 mL
Pink grapefruit juice	2/3 cup	150 mL
Can of mandarin orange segments		
(10 oz., 284 mL), with juice		
Ice cubes	6	6
Gin, optional	6 tbsp.	90 mL
Grenadine syrup	1/2 tsp.	2 mL
Lime slices	4	4

Citrus Cream: Process first 4 ingredients in blender until smooth.

Divide and measure gin and grenadine into 4 small chilled glasses. Pour Citrus Cream over top of each.

Garnish each with lime slice. Serves 4.

1 serving (with alcohol): 239 Calories; 2.1 g Total Fat (0.6 g Mono, 0.1 g Poly, 1.2 g Sat); 5 mg Cholesterol; 44 g Carbohydrate; trace Fibre; 2 g Protein; 52 mg Sodium

pineapple strawberry cocktail

Thick and fruity. Garnish with slice of strawberry and a chunk of pineapple on a skewer.

Pineapple juice	2 cups	500 mL
Vodka	1/2 cup	125 mL
Orange-flavoured liqueur (such as Cointreau)	1/2 cup	125 mL
Frozen strawberries	2 cups	500 mL
Lime juice	1 tbsp.	15 mL

Process all 5 ingredients in a blender until smooth. Serves 4.

1 serving: 210 Calories; 0 g Total Fat (0 g Mono, 0 g Poly, 0 g Sat); 0 mg Cholesterol; 28 g Carbohydrate; 2 g Fibre; trace Protein; 0 mg Sodium

tropical cream liqueur

Thick and creamy, this rum and pineapple-flavoured liqueur can be savoured as is, or pour 1 or 2 ounces over ice in a medium glass and fill the glass with orange juice or lemon-lime soft drink.

Can of crushed pineapple (14 oz., 398 mL), with juice	1	1
Ripe medium bananas (see Tip, page 64)	2	2
Lime juice	1 tsp.	5 mL
Can of coconut cream (14 oz., 398 mL)	1	1
Can of sweetened condensed milk (11 oz., 300 mL)	1	1
Cans of evaporated milk (13 1/2 oz., 385 mL)	2	2
Bottle of white (light) rum (13 1/4 oz., 375 mL)	1	1
Bottle of vodka (13 1/4 oz., 375 mL)	1	1

Process pineapple with juice, bananas and lime juice in blender or food processor until smooth.

Add coconut cream and condensed milk. Process for about 1 minute until well combined. Transfer to large bowl.

Add evaporated milk, rum and vodka. Stir well. Chill overnight. Stir. Pour into sterile jars or decorative bottles with tight-fitting lids. Store in refrigerator for up to 1 month. Makes about 8 1/2 cups (2.1 L).

1 oz. (30 mL): 82 Calories; 3.4 g Total Fat (0.5 g Mono, 0.1 g Poly, 2.6 g Sat); 5 mg Cholesterol; 6 g Carbohydrate; trace Fibre; 1 g Protein; 20 mg Sodium

irish cream

Homemade Irish cream beats store-bought any day. You'll be amazed at how easy it is to create a fancy liqueur.

Canadian whisky (rye)	1 1/2 cups	375 mL
Can of sweetened condensed milk	1	1
(11 oz., 300 mL)		
Half-and-half cream	1 cup	250 mL
Large eggs	2	2
Chocolate milk powder	1 tsp.	5 mL
Instant coffee granules	1 tsp.	5 mL
Vanilla extract	1 tsp.	5 mL

Put all 7 ingredients into blender. Process until smooth. Pour into sterile glass jar with tight-fitting lid. Chill. Makes about 4 1/2 cups (1.1 L).

1 oz. (30 mL): 73 Calories; 2.1 g Total Fat (0.5 g Mono, 0.1 g Poly, 1.2 g Sat); 19 mg Cholesterol; 7 g Carbohydrate; 0 g Fibre; 1 g Protein; 22 mg Sodium

peanut butter blast

A rich, creamy peanut butter, chocolate and banana milkshake. The kids will love this one.

Milk	1 1/2 cups	375 mL
Chocolate ice cream	1 cup	250 mL
Frozen ripe medium banana (see Tip, page 64)	1	1
Smooth (or crunchy) peanut butter	1 tbsp.	15 mL

Process all 4 ingredients in blender until smooth. Makes about 3 1/2 cups (875 mL). Pour into 4 chilled small glasses. Serves 4.

1 serving: 167 Calories; 7.1 g Total Fat (2.4 g Mono, 0.8 g Poly, 3.5 g Sat); 16 mg Cholesterol; 22 g Carbohydrate; 1 g Fibre; 6 g Protein; 94 mg Sodium

pbaj smoothie

Peanut butter, amaranth and jam would be good in a sandwich but are splendid in a smoothie.

Amaranth, toasted (see Tip, page 64)	3 tbsp.	45 mL
Milk	1 cup	250 mL
Vanilla yogurt	1/2 cup	125 mL
Smooth peanut butter	1/4 cup	60 mL
Raspberry jam	3 tbsp.	45 mL

Put amaranth into blender. Process until finely ground.

Add remaining 4 ingredients. Process until smooth. Makes about 2 cups (500 mL).

1 cup (250 mL): 436 Calories; 19.8 g Total Fat (8.4 g Mono, 5.0 g Poly, 4.9 g Sat); 8 mg Cholesterol; 52 g Carbohydrate; 4 g Fibre; 17 g Protein; 104 mg Sodium

peach chi chi

A milder variation of a popular drink. A small section of fresh pineapple makes the perfect garnish. For an adult version, add 1/4 cup (60 mL) of vodka.

Unsweetened pineapple juice	2/3 cup	150 mL
Coconut cream	6 tbsp.	90 mL
Ripe fresh peach, peeled	1	1
(or 2 canned peach halves), cut up		
Ginger ale	1 cup	250 mL

Put all 4 ingredients into blender. Process for 30 seconds. Makes 2 2/3 cups (650 mL). Serves 2.

1 serving: 200 Calories; 10 g Total Fat (0 g Mono, 0 g Poly, 9 g Sat); 0 mg Cholesterol; 28 g Carbohydrate; 2 g Fibre; 2 g Protein; 40 mg Sodium

chocolate orange drink

Who doesn't love the combination of chocolate and orange? Rich and satisfying.

Orange juice	1 cup	250 mL
Cocoa, sifted	1 tbsp.	15 mL
Granulated sugar	1 tbsp.	15 mL
Vanilla	1/8 tsp.	0.5 mL
Crushed ice	1/2 cup	125 mL

Combine all 5 ingredients in blender. Process until smooth. Pour over crushed ice. Makes 1 2/3 cups (400 mL). Serves 3.

1 serving: 60 Calories; 0 g Total Fat (0 g Mono, 0 g Poly, 0 g Sat); 0 mg Cholesterol; 13 g Carbohydrate; <1 g Fibre; 1 g Protein; 0 mg Sodium

cinnamon-spiced milkshake

If you've never had a spicy milkshake, this is the one to try! Cinnamon and vanilla flavour a thick caramel shake.

Milk	2/3 cup	150 mL
Brown sugar, packed	1/4 cup	60 mL
Large marshmallows, quartered	6	6
Ground cinnamon	1/2 tsp.	2 mL
Vanilla ice cream	3 cups	750 mL
Milk	1 cup	250 mL

Measure first 4 ingredients into small saucepan. Heat and stir on medium until marshmallow is melted. Transfer to blender.

Add ice cream and second amount of milk. Process until smooth. Makes 5 1/2 cups (1/4 L). Serves 4.

1 serving: 251 Calories; 9.2 g Total Fat (2.7 g Mono, 0.3 g Poly, 5.7 g Sat); 37 mg Cholesterol; 39 g Carbohydrate; trace Fibre; 5 g Protein; 108 mg Sodium

peach lemonade

The tartness of lemonade is tempered with the fresh and summery taste of peaches in this sweet, yet balanced mocktail. For an adults-only twist, add 1 oz. (30 mL) white rum or peach schnapps to each serving.

Can of sliced peaches (14 oz., 398 mL), with syrup	**1**	**1**
Water	3 cups	750 mL
Lemon juice	1 cup	250 mL
Granulated sugar	1/2 cup	125 mL

Put peaches and syrup into blender. Process until smooth. Remove 1 cup (250 mL) peach purée. Set aside. Fill ice cube tray with remaining peach purée. Freeze until firm.

Combine remaining 3 ingredients in large pitcher. Add reserved peach purée. Stir. Just before serving, add frozen peach purée. Stir. Makes about 5 cups (1.25 L).

1 cup (250 mL): 122 Calories; trace Total Fat (trace Mono, trace Poly, 0 g Sat); 0 mg Cholesterol; 33 g Carbohydrate; 1 g Fibre; 1 g Protein; 4 mg Sodium

strawberry slush

A slushy summer favourite! The sweet juiciness of ripe strawberries with a tang of lime. Garnish individual servings with fresh whole strawberries for a lovely presentation.

Lemon lime soft drink	1 1/2 cups	375 mL
Frozen whole strawberries, cut up (about 15)	1 1/2 cups	375 mL
Crushed ice	1 cup	250 mL
Granulated sugar	1/4 cup	60 mL

Measure all 4 ingredients into blender. Process until smooth. Makes 2 2/3 cups (650 mL). Serves 2.

1 serving: 200 Calories; 0 g Total Fat (0 g Mono, 0 g Poly, 0 g Sat); 0 mg Cholesterol; 53 g Carbohydrate; 2 g Fibre; <1 g Protein; 20 mg Sodium

recipe index

Malted Banana Shake, 6
Mango Almond Smoothie, 12
Maple Iced Coffee, 32
Milkshake, Cinnamon-spiced, 56
Mixed Berry Smoothie, 16
Mocha Coffee, 30

Nut Butter Drinks
    Mango Almond Smoothie, 12
    PBAJ Smoothie, 50
    Peanut Butter Blast, 48

Orange Frostbite, 36

PBAJ Smoothie, 50
Peach Chi Chi, 52
Peach Lemonade, 58
Peanut Butter Blast, 48
Pineapple Strawberry Cocktail, 42

Rainforest Smoothie, 14

Shakes
    Berry Bran Shake, 18
    Cinnamon-spiced Milkshake, 56
    Citrus Shake, 2
    Coffee Alexander Shake, 34
    Malted Banana Shake, 6

Slush, Strawberry, 60
Smoothie(s)
    Blueberry Lemonade, 8
    Coconut Fruit, 4
    Gazpacho, 24
    Mango Almond, 12
    Mixed Berry, 16
    PBAJ, 50
    Rainforest, 14
    Strawberry Carrot, 26
Strawberry Carrot Smoothie, 26
Strawberry Slush, 60
Sunburst, Citrus, 40

Tea Drinks
    Wake-up Call, 20
Tropical Cream Liqueur, 44

Vegetable Drinks
    Gazpacho Smoothie, 24
    Green Chill, 22
    Lime Cucumber Lassi, 28
    Strawberry Carrot Smoothie, 26

Wake-up Call, 20

topical tips

Cold strong coffee: When a recipe calls for cold strong coffee, try using espresso for an even stronger coffee flavour.

Cutting dates: Cutting dates with a knife can be a nuisance, but a good pair of kitchen shears makes light work of the task. Dip the blades of the shears in hot water to keep the fruit from sticking.

How to get coconut water from coconut: To get the coconut water out of a coconut, cut the husk off the bottom to expose the harder shell. You'll see 3 eyes. Punch holes in 2 eyes with a sharp object like a screwdriver or corkscrew (one will be soft enough to poke through easily, the other one will be harder). Turn upside down and drain the water from the coconut through a sieve (or drain, then strain) to get any bits of shell out.

Ripe bananas: When your bananas get too ripe to enjoy fresh, peel and cut them into 2 inch (5 cm) chunks and arrange in a single layer on a baking sheet. Freeze until firm. Store in a resealable freezer bag. Use 4 pieces for 1 medium banana.

Toasting grains: To toast grains, put them in a shallow frying pan. Heat on medium for about 5 minutes, stirring often, until golden. Remember not to toast more than one type of grain at a time because some types may take longer to toast than others.

Nutrition Information Guidelines

Each recipe is analyzed using the Canadian Nutrient File from Health Canada, which is based on the United States Department of Agriculture (USDA) Nutrient Database.

- If more than one ingredient is listed (such as "butter or hard margarine"), or if a range is given (1–2 tsp., 5–10 mL), only the first ingredient or first amount is analyzed.

- For meat, poultry and fish, the serving size per person is based on the recommended 4 oz. (113 g) uncooked weight (without bone), which is 2–3 oz. (57–85 g) cooked weight (without bone)— approximately the size of a deck of playing cards.

- Milk used is 1% M.F. (milk fat), unless otherwise stated.

- Cooking oil used is canola oil, unless otherwise stated.

- Ingredients indicating "sprinkle," "optional" or "for garnish" are not included in the nutrition information.

- The fat in recipes and combination foods can vary greatly depending on the sources and types of fats used in each specific ingredient. For these reasons, the count of saturated, monounsaturated and polyunsaturated fats may not add up to the total fat content.